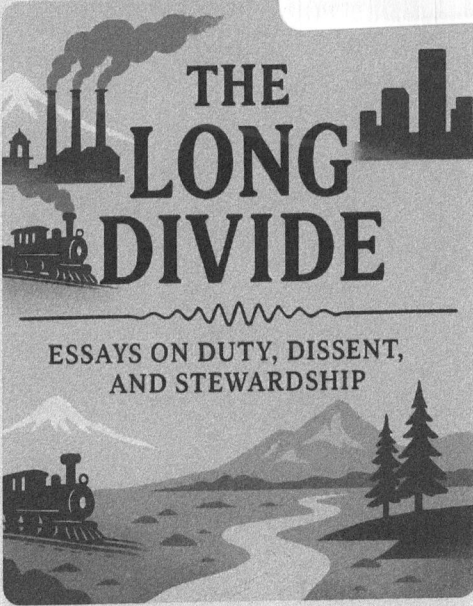

THE LONG DIVIDE

ESSAYS ON DUTY, DISSENT, AND STEWARDSHIP

CHRIS BURNETTE

ESSAYS ON DUTY, DISSENT, AND STEWARDSHIP

CONTENTS

The Long Divide

Essays on Duty, Dissent, and Stewardship

Volume 1

By Chris Burnette

El Burno Publishing
An imprint of El Burno Productions, Ltd.

Published by El Burno Publishing, an imprint of El Burno Productions, Ltd.
Fort Collins, Colorado
www.elburno.com

ISBNs:
Hard Cover: 978-1-967976-07-2
Paperback: 978-1-967976-08-9
Ebook: 978-1-967976-09-6
Audiobook: 978-1-967976-10-2

Printed in the United States of America

Cover design by El Burno Studios.
Interior design and typesetting by El Burno Studios

For permission requests, contact info@elburno.com

DEDICATION

For those who keep showing up.

FOREWORD

A republic is not a place. It is a posture.

We stand inside it every day. We shape it through our choices and our neglect.

When I started writing *The Long Divide*, I wasn't trying to build a manifesto. I was trying to understand what service means once the uniform comes off, once the mission ends, once the bureaucracy stops pretending to be noble. What remains after that? Duty. Conscience. The belief that integrity still matters, even when it is inconvenient.

These essays were written across many transitions: soldier to civilian, ranger to attorney, public servant to citizen. Each one captures a lesson that refused to fade. Stewardship is not ownership. It is guardianship. Whether you defend a park, a law, or an idea, the goal is the same. Leave it better than you found it.

This book is not for politicians or pundits. It is for the quiet professionals who keep the lights on, the files straight, and the public safe. It is for anyone who has looked at a failing institution and thought, *I can't fix it all, but I can keep this one corner honest.*

If these pages do their job, they will remind you that citizenship is a verb. The republic does not live in Washington. It lives wherever someone decides to do the right thing when no one is watching.

— Chris Burnette
Columbia, South Carolina
November 2025

PUBLISHER'S NOTE

From El Burno Publishing Ltd.

The Long Divide inaugurates our civic essay series dedicated to exploring conscience, leadership, and public service in modern democracy. These reflections by attorney and veteran Chris Burnette examine what it means to serve with integrity when institutions falter. The collection embodies our mission to publish works that strengthen civic stewardship through reason, courage, and hope. You can find audio versions of these essays, and others, at www.elburno.com.

TABLE OF CONTENTS

THE QUIET LINE WE HOLD

from The Long Divide: Essays on Duty, Dissent, and Stewardship

There is a moment every public servant faces. Whether in uniform, behind a desk, or out on the trail, it comes when you realize that duty is not about obedience. It is about conscience.

That realization came to me slowly. It happened in small rooms where good people convinced themselves that silence was professionalism. It happened in meetings where the truth was softened for comfort. It happened in briefings where numbers were adjusted to fit politics instead of people. That is where I learned what loyalty really costs.

We like to believe the republic sustains itself. We imagine it running on the same invisible current that keeps the lights on and the mail moving. It doesn't. Democracy depends on conscience. It survives because ordinary people, spread across offices and towns, keep doing the right thing when no one is watching.

I have spent most of my life in service to systems: military, bureaucratic, and legal. Each one has the same flaw. None can save itself from moral decay.

Laws cannot fix cowardice. Procedures cannot replace courage. Mission statements cannot enforce integrity. The only defense against collapse is the character of the people inside.

That is what this book is about. The republic is not an institution. It is a decision. It is the daily choice to serve, to speak, and to act with integrity, even when it costs you something.

In the Air Force, I learned that power without restraint is only motion without direction. In the Park Service, I learned that stewardship is more than conservation. It is the habit of leaving something better than you found it. In the law, I learned that justice does not sustain itself. It must be repaired again and again.

We live in a time that mistakes volume for virtue and spectacle for strength. The loudest voices dominate while the people holding the line are too busy doing their jobs to explain themselves. They are the ones who keep the country from collapsing under the weight of its own noise.

Each generation has to decide whether decency still counts as a public virtue. That choice is not made at the ballot box. It is made in classrooms, offices, and neighborhoods. It is made when one person refuses to cut corners, falsify data, or excuse cruelty. These decisions are invisible to history, but they are essential to freedom.

The republic does not fail when enemies attack it. It

fails when its stewards forget why it exists.

I wrote this book for the people who have not forgotten. The ones who hold the quiet line between what is easy and what is right. They do not ask for recognition, and they rarely get it. Yet they are the ones who keep democracy alive.

You will not find them on campaign posters or in viral videos. You will find them in the ranger who clears a trail before dawn, in the analyst who tells the truth when it is inconvenient, in the teacher who refuses to give up on a student everyone else has written off.

This book is for them. For the unseen republics within us all. For the people who still believe that stewardship is a form of rebellion, that truth still matters, and that freedom must be earned by conscience, not by comfort.

In the end, the line we hold is not between parties or ideologies. It is between those who serve the truth and those who serve themselves.

That line, fragile and often invisible, is the only thing that keeps the republic alive.

THE OATH AND THE SILENCE

from The Long Divide: Essays on Duty, Dissent, and Stewardship

Every oath begins the same way. You stand straight, raise your hand, and speak words written long before you were born. You swear to defend something larger than yourself. You do not yet understand what that promise will cost.

When I took my first oath, I thought it was about loyalty. Later, I learned it was about restraint. To defend a nation, or a principle, means you must know where power ends and conscience begins. Most of us learn that only after we've crossed the line once or twice and had to live with what that felt like.

Every profession that serves the public has its own version of the oath. The soldier's oath. The ranger's creed. The attorney's pledge. All share the same promise: that duty is not a weapon and service is not self-promotion. An oath binds you to principle, not personality. It does not belong to the person in charge. It belongs to the idea of the republic itself.

Keeping that promise is harder than taking it. The real test comes later, in silence. It happens when you see something wrong and have to decide whether to speak. It happens when the easy answer conflicts with the honest one. It happens when someone tells you to let it go and you know that letting go would mean betraying what you swore to protect.

I have watched people break under that pressure. Good people. They did not set out to fail. They just stopped fighting small battles until their silence became a habit. That is how decay spreads in any institution: one quiet compromise at a time.

When I worked in government, I saw how many policies depended not on law but on conscience. The regulations were clear, yet the outcomes always hinged on one person's willingness to say no. The system works only as long as someone inside still believes that truth is not optional.

Breaking silence does not always mean going public. Sometimes it means refusing to participate in the lie. Sometimes it means writing the accurate version of an event even if you know it will be buried. Sometimes it means standing your ground long enough that the next person has a chance to do the same.

We talk about courage as if it lives only in dramatic moments, but most courage happens in quiet rooms where no one is watching. It is the courage to stay honest when compromise would be safer. It is the courage to stay kind when cruelty has become fashionable. It is the courage to keep faith with your oath when others have stopped believing in theirs.

Silence has its place. It can be discipline. It can be respect. But when silence protects corruption, it becomes complicity. The oath does not end when your shift ends or when you leave the service. It follows you home. It shapes every decision that touches another life.

The uniform gave me discipline. The bureaucracy gave me perspective. But disillusionment gave me conviction. Once you have seen how fragile integrity can be, you understand why the republic cannot survive without people willing to defend it quietly, steadfastly, and without applause.

So I still carry that oath like an order, one that does not expire. Hold the line. Tell the truth. And when silence feels safer than honesty, speak anyway.

THE RANGER AND THE REPUBLIC

from The Long Divide: Essays on Duty, Dissent, and Stewardship

The Air Force taught me discipline. The Park Service taught me reverence. Not the ceremonial kind, but the kind that humbles you when the wind moves through the trees and you realize the land doesn't need you at all. It simply endures.

Working for the National Park Service changed my understanding of authority. In the military, you defend a flag. In the parks, you defend everything beneath it—the ground, the water, and the memory of what came before. You become a custodian of something older than the nation itself.

Stewardship is not glamorous. It is often cold, muddy, and thankless. It is trail work in the rain, wildfire briefings before dawn, and long phone calls with angry communities. It is the slow, deliberate work of caretaking. Balancing access and protection. Progress and permanence.

For years, I walked the boundary between policy and wilderness. One foot in bureaucracy. One foot in the backcountry. Some days I negotiated budgets.

Other days I shoveled snow off bridges or cleared rockslides from roads. Somewhere in that rhythm, I learned what service really meant.

The Park Service has a quiet creed: *For the benefit and enjoyment of the people.* Those words are carved in stone at the Roosevelt Arch in Yellowstone. They sound noble, but they also read like a warning. "For the people" does not mean "for our convenience." It means for our stewardship, for our duty to protect what we did not create.

The same is true of the republic. Freedom is not a resource to be consumed. It is a landscape to be maintained. Democracy, like wilderness, erodes when neglected. It does not collapse overnight. It fades through small acts of carelessness and the comfort of assuming someone else is tending the trail.

I have met people in the parks who understood that instinctively. Maintenance workers who picked up trash no one else would see. Volunteers who cleared storm debris before sunrise. Interpreters who told the hard parts of history even when visitors winced. They understood that preservation is not passive. It is a form of devotion.

The same kind of devotion keeps a democracy alive. It is the quiet discipline of people who fix what others ignore, mend what is frayed, and tell the truth when it would be easier to stay silent.

The work of a ranger is not that different from the work of a citizen. Both are trusted with something fragile, precious, and incomplete. Both inherit their duty from those who came before. Both are expected to leave it better for those who will follow. That is stewardship in its purest form.

In the field, rangers follow a simple rule: *Leave no trace.* It is meant for hikers, but I think of it as a civic principle. The goal is not to leave no mark. It is to leave no wound. To make sure your presence adds stability instead of harm.

If the republic feels fragile, it is not because it has failed. It is because too many people have forgotten that citizenship, like conservation, is maintenance. It is the hard, unglamorous labor of care. It is the discipline of showing up, again and again, to do the work no one else wants to do.

The ranger's creed and the citizen's creed are essentially the same. Protect what is worth keeping. Repair what has been damaged. Leave it better than you found it.

That is how you serve a republic. That is how you serve the land.

THE PAPER SHIELD

from The Long Divide: Essays on Duty, Dissent, and Stewardship

For all the ceremony we give it, the Constitution is still just paper. Ink and parchment. Fragile. Flammable. It has no power unless people choose to honor it. That is the uncomfortable truth about freedom. It survives not through permanence, but through participation.

I did not learn that in law school. I learned it inside government offices where the words of that document either live in practice or die in procedure. The Constitution is not a shield of perfection. It is a mirror. It reflects the integrity of whoever holds it.

The bureaucracy, for all its flaws, is where the Constitution lives or fails. On its best days, it hums with quiet purpose: dedicated people translating laws into services and policies into protections. On its worst days, it becomes a fog that hides accountability. Most citizens never see that side. They imagine "the government" as one machine. Inside, it is a living system of conscience, some parts healthy, others infected, all dependent on who is tending the garden.

The paper shield only works if those holding it refuse to bend. I have seen how narrow the line can be between lawful order and ethical collapse. Sometimes it is one person in a meeting who refuses to sign a bad order. Sometimes it is a lawyer who insists on accuracy when a supervisor demands speed. Those are not moments of heroism. They are moments of endurance.

Every federal employee takes the same oath: to support and defend the Constitution. It is not a ritual. It is a tether that ties conscience to duty. The challenge is that the document we swear to uphold cannot enforce itself. It relies on interpretation, restraint, and the courage to say no when the letter of the law collides with its spirit.

As an attorney, I see the Constitution differently now. It is not a relic to be worshiped or a weapon to be wielded. It is a contract to be maintained. A fragile agreement among imperfect people who promise to govern themselves. It is sacred not because it is perfect, but because it dares to trust us with freedom.

That trust is the foundation of the American experiment. The Founders did not create a self-executing democracy. They built a framework that depends entirely on human integrity. Every clause and every amendment assumes that enough people will act honorably enough of the time to keep the whole thing standing.

The law is often called a sword or a shield. I think of the Constitution as something simpler. It is a compass. It does not move on its own, but it always points true. Ignore it long enough, and you drift.

When I left government service, I hung a copy of the Constitution on my office wall. Not for decoration. For accountability. It is there to remind me that justice does not live in that paper. It lives in the people who interpret it.

The Constitution is a remarkable invention, but it was never meant to do the work for us. It cannot save us from apathy or fear. It can only give us a place to stand while we decide whether we still believe in the principles it represents.

It is, in the end, a paper shield. But it will hold, if we keep holding it up.

THE MINISTRY OF COWARDS

from The Long Divide: Essays on Duty, Dissent, and Stewardship

There was a time when leadership meant risk. To hold office or command meant you might lose something for the sake of doing what was right. Somewhere along the way, that meaning was reversed. Today, leadership often means insulation. It means finding ways to avoid consequence. It means surrounding yourself with buffers until the truth can no longer reach you.

The problem with our institutions is not that they are full of villains. It is that they are full of cowards. Decent, educated, capable people who know what is right but refuse to act because the cost might be personal. They whisper the truth in private and perform neutrality in public. They call it professionalism. I call it surrender.

I have watched this disease spread through agencies, nonprofits, and corporations alike. It hides behind procedure and branding. It uses language like "staying in our lane," "protecting the mission," and "not getting political." These are not strategies. They are disguises for fear. Fear of losing funding. Fear of losing status. Fear of being the first to say what everyone already knows.

Bureaucracy rewards timidity. It mistakes delay for diligence and consensus for wisdom. When you are surrounded by careerists, courage becomes an administrative inconvenience. I have sat in meetings where integrity was treated as a variable to be managed. The rot does not announce itself. It arrives dressed as caution.

I remember a supervisor who buried an internal report because the findings would have embarrassed leadership. It was not illegal. It was just cowardly. The truth was inconvenient, so it was quietly edited out of existence. The justification was simple: "We need to stay focused on the mission." That phrase has excused more moral failure than any ideology in history.

The real problem is not corruption. It is fear. We have built a culture that confuses safety with virtue. Safety has never built anything worth keeping. Every meaningful advance in our history—moral, scientific, or political—has come from someone who risked standing alone.

Leadership without courage is administration. Administration without integrity is decay. And decay, once normalized, becomes ideology.

That is how democracies fail. Not by invasion or revolution, but by the slow corrosion of character inside the very institutions that were created to protect them.

I have met the exceptions. They still exist in every organization. The ones who act like leadership is service. The manager who signs the memo no one else will. The inspector who refuses to dilute a finding. The advocate who tells the client the hard truth. They are reminders that courage still exists, even if it survives in isolation.

We do not need louder leaders. We need braver ones. People who value truth more than comfort and accountability more than applause. The republic does not need heroes. It needs stewards—men and women willing to lose something so the rest of us do not lose everything.

The cure for cowardice is not anger. It is an example. It is the quiet defiance of one person who refuses to play along. Courage spreads, but only if someone goes first.

So go first. Reject the culture of caution that mistakes silence for professionalism. Remember that every title and every office means nothing if it can only be exercised in comfort.

The work of leadership is not to preserve your position. It is to preserve your conscience.

If that costs you something, it means you are doing it right.

THE TWO AMERICAS

from The Long Divide: Essays on Duty, Dissent, and Stewardship

Every generation inherits two nations. One is drawn on maps. The other is drawn in the mind. The first is shaped by rivers and borders. The second is shaped by memory, fear, and myth. The tension between them has always been our fault line.

I have seen that divide from altitude and from ground level. From Air Force flightlines. From federal field offices. From mountain trails where a ranger's truck is the only sign of government for a hundred miles. The division is not just political. It is cultural, spiritual, even ecological. One side moves faster. The other remembers longer.

Spend enough time crossing between them and you start to feel the distance in your bones. In one town, the word "federal" means protection. In another, it means intrusion. To one family, a ranger in uniform represents preservation. To another, he represents the land their grandfather lost. To some, progress means technology. To others, it means losing what made life worth living in the first place.

This is not a divide between red and blue. It is a

divide between rhythms. One half of the country lives by acceleration. The other by endurance. One believes in solving problems with innovation. The other believes in solving them with calloused hands. Both believe the other has forgotten what the country means.

After I left government service, I drove across the country often. What I saw was not division so much as exhaustion. Americans are tired of being told to hate each other. They just do not know how to stop. Outrage has become an industry, and fear its currency. Politicians who cannot build anything have learned to profit from destruction.

The republic, like the environment, erodes first at its edges. And yet, I have seen quiet resistance to that erosion. A veteran who stocks a food pantry instead of arguing online. A park superintendent who rebuilds trust with tribal leaders ignored for generations. A mayor who plants trees instead of billboards. They do not trend. They do not posture. But they are rebuilding the country in increments.

That is the truth about our two Americas. They are not enemies. They are estranged partners who forgot how to listen. Bridging the divide does not mean agreement. It means remembering that democracy is worth the effort of disagreement. It means telling the truth about our failures without surrendering to despair.

Every democracy is a relationship. It survives

only when someone keeps showing up after the argument.

If the first American experiment was about expansion, the second must be about repair. We have built enough walls. What we lack are caretakers—people willing to stand in the middle ground, take the arrows from both sides, and keep building anyway.

The divide will not close in my lifetime. But that is not the point. The point is to keep crossing it. To keep reminding whoever stands on the other side that the map is not the territory, and the republic is not the government. It is us.

THE HIDDEN NETWORK

from The Long Divide: Essays on Duty, Dissent, and Stewardship

Some of the most important work in this country happens off the record. It does not trend. It does not earn headlines. It does not come with awards. But it happens every day, in offices and classrooms, in labs and field stations, in the long shadow of institutions that have forgotten their purpose.

I think of the people who still show up and do the work anyway as the hidden network. They are not part of a movement or a party. They are a quiet fellowship of conscience. They do not advertise their beliefs because they are too busy living them. You will not find them on panels or in hashtags, but you can feel their presence wherever good work continues despite the odds.

They are the analysts who refuse to alter data to fit a narrative.

The teachers who keep history honest when others demand comfort.

The scientists who publish inconvenient results.

The lawyers who tell clients the truth instead of

what they want to hear.

The rangers who protect what cannot speak for itself.

They form the republic's unseen foundation, a network of integrity that stretches beneath every institution. They connect people who would never meet, yet share the same compass. They move truth quietly through systems that have forgotten how to hear it.

Every era of decline produces its own underground of decency. You rarely see it until the crisis has passed and someone asks how the whole thing didn't collapse. The answer is always the same. Someone, somewhere, kept doing their job right.

There is nothing romantic about this work. It is maintenance. It is slow, humble, and often unrewarded. It is done by people who hold to their ethics even when they are punished for it.

That is what resilience really means. It's not noise or defiance for its own sake. But discipline in the shadows.

Patriotism, in its truest form, is the decision to be reliable when everything around you becomes performative. This hidden network proves that a republic does not survive through laws alone. It survives through conscience, distributed across millions of ordinary choices.

When cynicism starts to feel like wisdom, I think of them. The colleagues, the neighbors, the strangers who keep fixing what others break. They are the living infrastructure of hope. They are proof that decency is not extinct, only underreported.

History will not remember their names, but it will rest on their shoulders. And if the republic endures, it will be because they did what citizens have always done when institutions falter. They kept faith. They kept working. They kept each other from forgetting why any of this mattered.

THE QUIET REBELLION

from The Long Divide: Essays on Duty, Dissent, and Stewardship

Revolutions make headlines. Rebellions rarely do. And yet, it is the quiet ones that last.

Most of my life has been spent inside institutions that talk about change but fear what it requires. They form committees, write strategies, and issue plans that orbit the same truth. They want transformation without discomfort. But real change never begins in a boardroom. It begins with one person who decides to stop pretending.

That decision is rebellion. Not the loud kind that thrives on outrage, but the quiet kind that grows out of conscience. It is the ranger who files the report everyone else ignores. The analyst who refuses to alter the numbers. The teacher who tells the truth about history. The attorney who takes the right case instead of the easy one. These people do not march or shout. They simply refuse to surrender their integrity. That refusal is a form of revolution.

I call it the quiet rebellion. It looks ordinary. It feels lonely. But it is the only force strong enough to outlast corruption.

We live in a time that confuses noise with influence. Anger travels faster than truth. Fear organizes more quickly than faith. Everyone is expected to choose a side, perform loyalty, and speak in slogans. But the republic will not be saved by the loudest voices. It will be saved by the most steadfast. By the ones who do their duty when no one is watching. By the ones who fix what is broken without needing applause.

Every failure of democracy begins small. A little dishonesty here. A little apathy there. The same is true of redemption. The cure for corruption is not ideology. It is example. Trust will return to our institutions only when the people inside them become trustworthy again.

The Founders never promised perfection. They gave us a framework built on faith—faith that free people could govern themselves and re-earn that right in every generation. Somewhere along the way, we mistook inheritance for entitlement. We started treating democracy like a subscription, renewed automatically.

The truth is harder, and nobler. The republic is not self-executing. It survives only when enough of us decide to act like citizens, not customers.

My quiet rebellion is simple. To live by the oath long after the uniform. To keep faith with ideals long after the applause. To treat service not as a career, but as a calling.

I have lost faith in plenty of institutions, but not in people. I have seen too much quiet goodness to accept cynicism as wisdom. The line still holds, though thinner than before. It holds because someone you will never meet is still doing their job right.

A clerk who refuses to shred evidence.
A ranger who still patches the trail.
A teacher who still tells the truth.
A lawyer who refuses to look away.

That is the rebellion. That is the republic.

And if we are lucky, it will be enough.

FOR THOSE WHO KEEP SHOWING UP

from The Long Divide: Essays on Duty, Dissent, and Stewardship

History does not bend on its own. It bends because someone, somewhere, refuses to let it stay crooked. Every generation produces a few people who understand that truth. They are not revolutionaries in the cinematic sense. They are the ones who keep the lights on in dark times, who show up early, stay late, and carry standards no one else is watching. Their names will never appear in headlines, but their fingerprints are on everything that endures.

This book began as a reflection on service, but it ends as a letter of gratitude. It is for those who keep the republic alive by treating ordinary work as sacred. The ranger who patches a washed-out trail. The clerk who files the record correctly when no one will check. The nurse who writes one more note before leaving her shift. The veteran who volunteers at a shelter. The citizen who votes even when it feels pointless.

They do not see themselves as heroes, and that is exactly why they are. They understand something too many have forgotten. The republic is not an abstraction. It is a shared obligation, renewed each day by the people who choose to do their jobs with integrity.

Some days that feels like enough. Other days it feels like bailing out the ocean with a bucket. But progress is cumulative. Every act of decency adds weight to the right side of the scale.

We are taught to believe that heroism lives in the extraordinary. The truth is harder, and simpler. Most of the republic's defenders are quiet people doing ordinary things well. They are the ones who pick up the litter others drop, who correct the record when lies spread, who still believe that public service is honorable.

They rarely make speeches. They simply keep showing up. That, more than any monument or slogan, is what keeps this country standing. The daily, unglamorous faith that truth and decency still matter, even when the world forgets.

If you are tired, you are not alone. If you wonder whether it is worth it, it is. Somewhere, someone you will never meet is holding their corner of the line, just as you are holding yours. Together, even unseen, we make a republic.

For those who keep showing up—thank you. You are the reason this still works.

ACKNOWLEDGMENTS

For the mentors, colleagues, and citizens who taught me that integrity is its own reward.

For Elise, whose courage and patience have made every good thing possible.

And for my children, who remind me daily why the republic must endure.

ABOUT THE AUTHOR

Chris Burnette is an attorney, veteran, and former National Park Service leader whose work explores the intersection of public service, conscience, and democracy. He writes and records from Columbia, South Carolina, continuing to produce books, essays, and civic media through El Burno Publishing Ltd. and El Burno Studios.

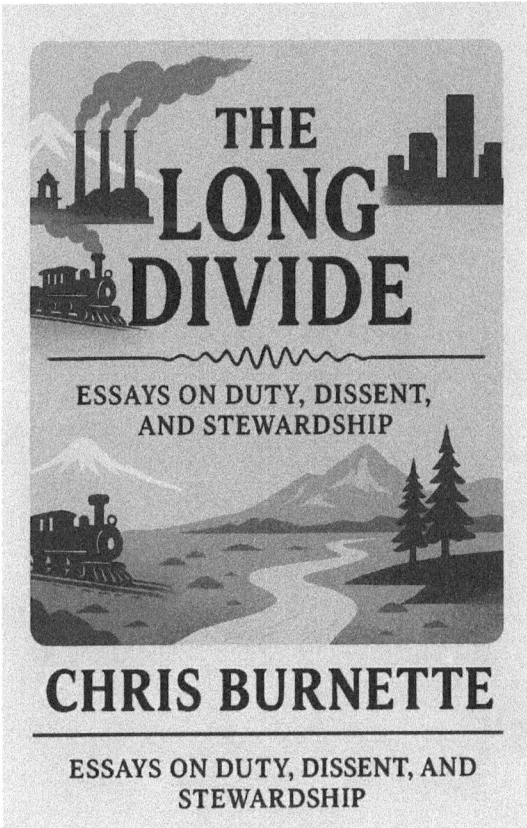

THE LONG DIVIDE

ESSAYS ON DUTY, DISSENT, AND STEWARDSHIP

CHRIS BURNETTE

ESSAYS ON DUTY, DISSENT, AND STEWARDSHIP

El Burno Publishing, an imprint of El Burno Productions, Ltd.

www.ingramcontent.com/pod-product-compliance
Lightning Source LLC
Chambersburg PA
CBHW060531280326
41933CB00014B/3131